YOUR PASSPORT TO SWEDEN

by Nancy Dickmann

CAPSTONE PRESS
a capstone imprint

Published by Capstone Press, an imprint of Capstone
1710 Roe Crest Drive, North Mankato, Minnesota 56003
capstonepub.com

Library of Congress Cataloging-in-Publication Data is available on the Library of Congress website.
ISBN: 9798875245879 (hardcover)
ISBN: 9798875245824 (paperback)
ISBN: 9798875245831 (ebook PDF)

Summary: What is it like to live in or visit Sweden? What makes Sweden's culture unique? Explore the sights and daily lives of Swedish people.

Editorial Credits
Editor: Elaine Duncan; Designer: Sarah Bennett; Media Researcher: Rebekah Hubstenberger; Production Specialist: Tori Abraham

Image Credits
Capstone Press: Eric Gohl, 5; Getty Images: Adam Pretty, 26, David Clapp, 15, DEA PICTURE LIBRARY, 28, georgeclerk, 16, iStock/Jazzanna, 8, iStock/klug-photo, 9 (top right), iStock/Reimphoto, 23, iStock/yes-thats-it, 14 (top), Johner Images, 6, Malcolm P Chapman, 20, Mats Brynolf, 14 (bottom), Matthias Hangst, 27,Omar Havana, 11, Westend61, 13; Shutterstock: Alexanderstock23, 18, Denklim, 9 (bottom right), Fotos593, 25, Isabelle Nyrot, 17, Lasse Johansson, 12, paolo airenti, 19, RPBaiao, 24, trabantos, front cover

Design Elements
Getty Images: iStock/Yevhenii Dubinko; Shutterstock: Flipser, Ivan Alex Burchak, Lightleak Creative, Net Vector, pingebat

Printed and bound in Malaysia. 006460

CONTENTS

Words in **bold** are in the glossary.

CHAPTER ONE

WELCOME TO SWEDEN!

Tall, old buildings line the cobbled streets. Many are painted in warm shades of orange and yellow. People walk together through the narrow streets. There are cafés, shops, museums, and galleries. This is Gamla Stan in Sweden. It's the oldest part of the capital city, Stockholm. Most of the buildings are hundreds of years old.

Sweden is a country in northern Europe. It is part of a region called Scandinavia. More than 10 million people live here. Sweden has many historic sites. It also has natural beauty. There are lakes, mountains, beaches, and national parks. Tourists come to enjoy the outdoors.

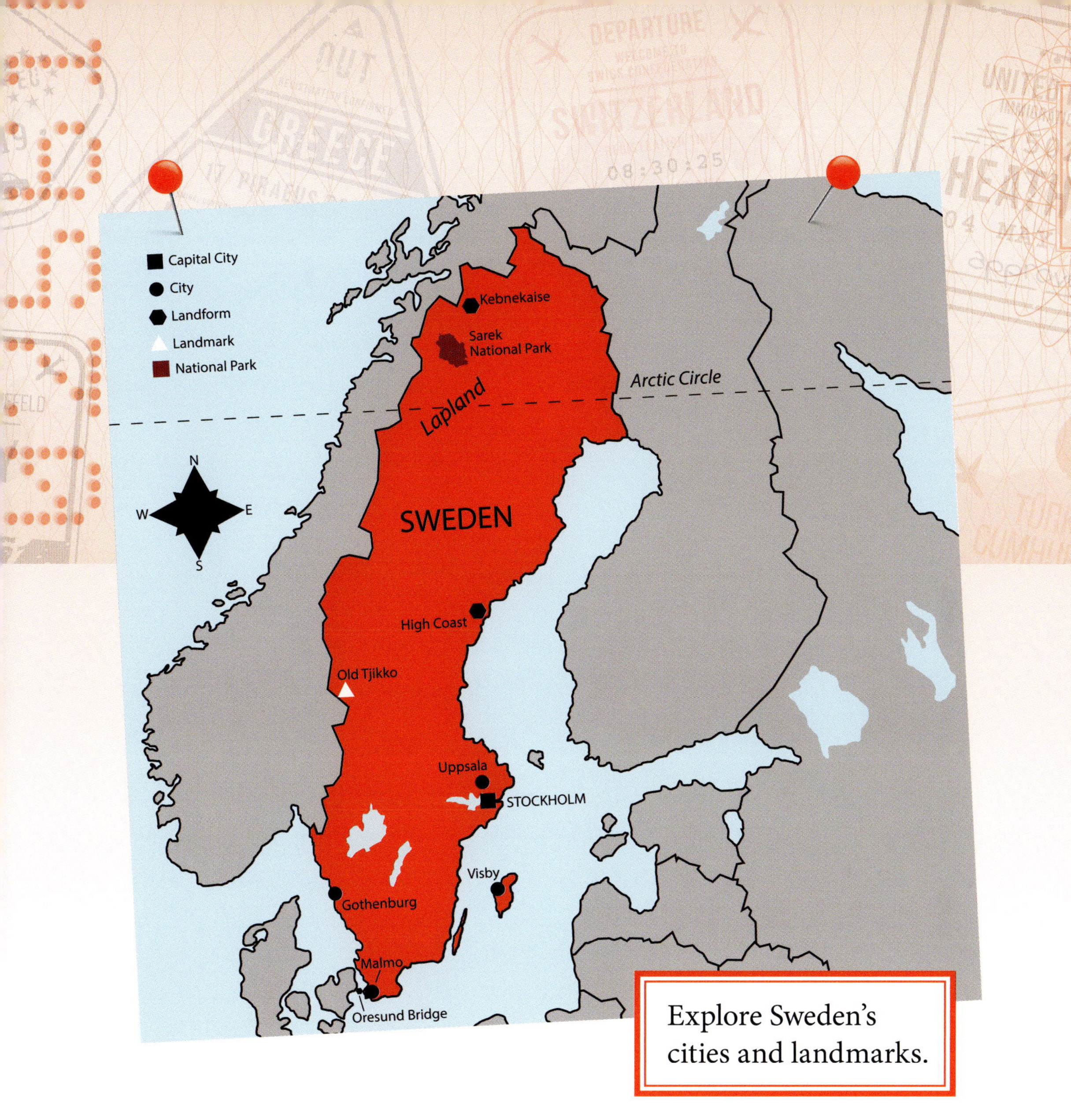

Explore Sweden's cities and landmarks.

Stockholm is built on 14 islands connected by more than 50 bridges.

ISLAND NATION

Many small islands cluster along Sweden's coast. Sweden has more islands than any other country. There are more than 250,000! Fewer than 1,000 of Sweden's islands have people living on them. Most people live on the mainland. Sweden also has thousands of lakes. The islands and lakes were carved by **glaciers**. The glaciers melted about 10,000 years ago. Their water filled the lakes.

FACT FILE

OFFICIAL NAME: .... KINGDOM OF SWEDEN

POPULATION: 10,647,157

LAND AREA: .... 158,431 SQ. MI. (410,335 SQ KM)

CAPITAL: .... STOCKHOLM

MONEY: .... SWEDISH KRONA

GOVERNMENT: .... PARLIAMENTARY CONSTITUTIONAL MONARCHY

LANGUAGES: .... SWEDISH (ALSO FINNISH, SÁMI, ROMANI, YIDDISH, AND MEÄNKIELI)

GEOGRAPHY: Sweden is on a peninsula in northern Europe. It borders Norway to the west, Finland to the east, and Denmark to the south. There are many small coastal islands.

NATURAL RESOURCES: Sweden produces a lot of hydroelectric power. It also produces iron, copper, lead, and timber.

LAND OF VIKINGS

About 1,200 years ago, Sweden was home to Vikings. They sailed around Europe, trading with some lands and raiding others. Today, Swedish people are known for being calm and polite. They are relaxed and **independent**. They value **equality** and fairness. For Swedes, work-life balance is important.

CHAPTER TWO

HISTORY OF SWEDEN

People have been living in Sweden since the ice covering it melted. This process began nearly 15,000 years ago. It took several thousand years. These early settlers used spears and bows and arrows to hunt moose, deer, and seals. They fished and gathered plants to eat. Later, they built homes, farms, and ships. Swedish traders traveled far. They bought and sold metals and other goods.

Some of the rock carvings in Tanum, Sweden, are more than 3,700 years old.

VIKINGS AND BEYOND

The Viking Age began around 800 CE. Sweden was not a united country. Local chiefs ruled in different areas. But, Sweden joined with the kingdoms of Norway and Finland to form a union in 1397. Queen Margaret of Denmark set up this union and Erik of Pomerania was crowned king. These kingdoms remained a union until they broke apart in 1523. Gustav Vasa was elected the king of Sweden.

By about 1100 CE, most people in Sweden had become Christian. They built large churches like the Lund Cathedral.

FACT

Sweden's flag is blue with a gold cross. One legend says that this is because of King Eric IX. In 1157, he led his army to invade Finland and saw a golden cross in the sky. Some people believe the flag shows this legend.

RISE AND FALL OF AN EMPIRE

In the 1600s, Sweden became an important power. It fought and won wars. This allowed Sweden to take over nearby lands. They included parts of present-day Russia, Germany, and Estonia. Sweden now had an **empire**. But by 1721, Sweden had started losing wars. It lost its territories. After that, Sweden's **parliament** forced the king to share power with them. In the 1800s, parliament made many new laws. They granted religious freedom and improved rights for women.

MODERN SWEDEN

During the empire, it seemed like Sweden was always at war. Now it is a peaceful country. Sweden did not take sides in World War I (1914–1918) or World War II (1939–1945). For a long time, Sweden did not form **alliances** with other countries. But in 1995, it joined the European Union to help the country's **economy**. After Russia **invaded** Ukraine in 2022, Sweden worried that it might be next. In 2024, it joined the North Atlantic Treaty Organization (NATO). This group of countries have agreed to help defend each other.

TIMELINE OF SWEDISH HISTORY

ABOUT 9000 BCE: The first humans arrive in what is now Sweden.

ABOUT 1000 BCE: People from Sweden trade with groups in central Europe.

ABOUT 800 CE: Vikings from Sweden begin to raid settlements in other lands.

ABOUT 1100: Most people in Sweden have converted to Christianity.

1167: Knut Eriksson becomes the king of all of Sweden.

1397: An official agreement unites Norway, Sweden, and Denmark under a single monarch.

1523: Norway, Sweden, and Denmark split up. Gustav Vasa becomes the king of Sweden.

EARLY 1600S: Sweden begins to take over new lands to form an empire.

EARLY 1700S: The Swedish Empire lost the lands it had conquered.

1814: This was the last time that Sweden fought a war with another country.

1818: A French general, Jean-Baptiste Bernadotte, is elected king of Sweden. His descendants still rule the country.

1914–18: During World War I, Sweden remains neutral.

1939–45: During World War II, Sweden remains neutral.

1953: A Swedish diplomat, Dag Hammarskjöld, becomes Secretary-General of the United Nations.

1995: Sweden joins the European Union.

2024: Sweden joins NATO.

A flag raising ceremony was held to mark Sweden joining NATO in 2024.

CHAPTER THREE

EXPLORE SWEDEN

Many parts of Sweden are wild and beautiful. People visit to enjoy nature. Forests cover more than two-thirds of the land. The most common trees are spruce and pine. People come to hike in the forests. They hope to see animals such as moose and lynx. Wolves, bears, and wolverines also live in the forests.

FACT

Old Tjikko is a Norway spruce tree. The trunk and branches are only a few hundred years old. But these parts keep regrowing from the same roots. The roots are nearly 10,000 years old!

Canoeing is a great way to explore Sweden's lakes.

LAND OF LAKES

Sweden has about 100,000 lakes. The largest is Lake Vänern. It is larger than Rhode Island. Sweden's peaceful lakes are popular vacation spots. People can swim, fish, or go kayaking. Visitors often camp or stay in rustic cabins. Some lakes have sandy beaches or bicycle paths around their shores. In winter, some of the lakes freeze. People can go ice-skating on their frozen waters.

Sweden has 30 national parks, including Sarek National Park in the rugged north.

MOUNTAINS AND SNOW

The Scandinavian Mountains run along Sweden's western border. Kebnekaise is Sweden's tallest mountain. It is part of this mountain range. Its peak stands 6,877 feet (2,096 meters) high. Some of the mountains are covered in snow year-round. People come to ski and snowboard in the winter. Deep valleys lie between the mountains. Animals such as arctic foxes live here.

Arctic fox

COASTAL BEAUTY

Sweden has about 2,000 miles (3,218 kilometers) of coastline. It lies mainly on the Baltic Sea and the Gulf of Bothnia. The bodies of water of the Kattegat and Skagerrak separate Sweden from Denmark and Norway. In the north, the coastline is rugged and beautiful. It is known as the High Coast. It's higher above sea level than most other coasts. This region has forests, mountains, and cliffs. There are old fishing villages and ancient rock carvings. In the south, the coastal areas are flatter. Many areas have sandy beaches.

THE NORTHERN LIGHTS

Sweden's far north lies inside the **Arctic Circle**. For several weeks in December, the sun never rises. Visitors ride a chairlift to the Aurora Sky Station. They hope to see shimmering lights in the sky. These "northern lights" can be green, blue, red, or pink.

Walking is a great way to explore the city of Stockholm.

STOCKHOLM

Stockholm is Sweden's capital. It is also its largest city. Many of its buildings are old. There are some modern buildings too. People get around on buses and the underground train system called the metro. Boats carry them between Stockholm's islands. The island of Djurgården has many museums. One has a wooden ship on display. It sank in 1628 and was raised in 1961.

FACT

Malmö is Sweden's third largest city. It lies across the water from Copenhagen, Denmark. A bridge and tunnel connect the two cities. The journey covers about 10 miles (16 km).

GOTHENBURG

Gothenburg, on the west coast, is Sweden's second largest city. Long ago, it was famous for fishing and shipbuilding. Now it is full of parks, museums, and cafés. Restaurants serve meals made from fresh local ingredients. The city is famous for seafood.

UPPSALA

Uppsala lies about 40 miles (65 km) north of Stockholm. Its university is one of Europe's oldest. Students make up about 20 percent of Uppsala's population. This gives the city a young, international vibe.

The town of Visby is on the island of Gotland. It has ancient buildings and old city walls.

CHAPTER FOUR

DAILY LIFE

Most people in Sweden live in cities. The south is more densely populated. Fewer people live in the north. Life in Sweden is relaxed and casual. People call each other by their first names, even their teachers and bosses. Some businesses shut down in July. This is when many Swedes go on vacation.

Families are important in Sweden. When people have a baby, each parent gets 240 days of paid time off. This lets them share the load of caring for their children. Education is free, even preschool and college. All students get a free hot meal at lunchtime.

Bikes are a popular way to get around. About 20 percent of people bike every day.

Sámi wear clothing with bright colors and patterns. These traditional clothes are called gákti.

THE SÁMI

The Sámi are an **Indigenous** group who live in Lapland. This area covers part of northern Sweden. It extends into Norway and Finland. The Sámi have lived on this land for thousands of years. They have their own language and culture. Many of them once herded reindeer, and some still do. At least 20,000 Sámi live in Sweden. They make crafts from natural materials such as wood and bone. These are often decorated with detailed patterns.

FOOD AND DRINK

Food is important in Swedish culture. People share meals with family and friends. Many people stop work in the morning for fika. This is a break for coffee and a sweet snack. Cinnamon buns are a popular choice. Fika is not just about food. Chatting and relaxing are just as important.

POPULAR DISHES

Swedish food is often made from local ingredients. Fish, pork, and potatoes are common. Foods such as herring and cucumber are often pickled. Many Swedish dishes are rich and hearty. Pea soup is popular. So are meatballs with mashed potatoes. Lingonberry jam is often served with food. Many families choose tacos for a Friday night treat.

People in Sweden often serve a smorgasbord at parties. This buffet has hot and cold dishes.

KLADDKAKA

This dessert has a name meaning "sticky cake." It's gooey, chocolatey, and delicious! The cake is often served with berries and ice cream or whipped cream.

Ingredients

- ½ cup butter
- 2 eggs
- 1 cup sugar
- 5 tablespoons unsweetened cocoa powder
- ⅔ cup all-purpose flour
- pinch of salt
- 1 teaspoon vanilla

Directions

1. Preheat the oven to 375°F.
2. Melt the butter in a pan or in the microwave. Set aside.
3. Beat the eggs and sugar until fluffy.
4. In a separate bowl, mix the cocoa powder, flour, and salt.
5. Stir these dry ingredients into the egg mixture. Then add the melted butter and vanilla.
6. Pour the batter into a greased 7–8 inch (18–20 centimeters) round baking pan.
7. Bake for 10 to 15 minutes. When the cake is done, it will look dry on top but wobble if you shake it gently.
8. Let the cake cool before removing it from the pan. Refrigerate until cool and serve.

CHAPTER FIVE

HOLIDAYS AND CELEBRATIONS

Christian holidays such as Christmas are important in Sweden. December 13 is St. Lucia Day. A girl wearing a white robe leads a **procession**. She wears a wreath of candles and passes out cookies and buns. The group includes other girls and boys dressed as stars or gingerbread men. At Christmas, people make gingerbread houses. Families give gifts and gather for a feast. They eat ham, smoked salmon, and other dishes.

FACT

Lent is the period before Easter. Before it starts, Swedes like to eat rich food. A spiced bun called a semla is very popular. It's filled with almond paste and whipped cream. Some people eat it in a bowl of hot milk.

People make Easter trees. They decorate twigs or bare trees with colored feathers and decorative paper eggs.

EASTER

Easter is another popular holiday. On one of the days before it, children dress as witches. They knock on doors to wish people a happy Easter. In return, they get candy. In some parts of Sweden, people light bonfires. On Easter, people eat pickled herring. They also have a salad made of eggs and fish.

VALBORG

Some Swedish festivals are hundreds of years old. Valborg is one of them. It is celebrated on April 30. People light bonfires and sing songs. In the past, this was to frighten evil spirits. Valborg marks the start of spring.

NATIONAL PRIDE

National Day is when Swedes celebrate their country. It takes place on June 6. This is the day that Gustav Vasa was elected king in 1523. On the same day in 1809, Sweden adopted a new **constitution**. People celebrate with flags and parades. There are ceremonies to welcome new citizens.

All Saints' Day is on a Saturday between October 31 and November 6. People light candles on their loved ones' graves.

A Midsummer celebration

MIDSUMMER

Midsummer is one of the most important holidays. It dates back many hundreds of years. Midsummer falls on June 20 or 21. This is the longest day of the year. Summer days are very long in Sweden. In Stockholm, the sun does not set until after 10 p.m. In the northern parts of the country, it doesn't set at all. People light fires and dance around a pole. They eat strawberries and other party foods. They play outdoor games and have sack races.

CHAPTER SIX

SPORTS AND RECREATION

Soccer is Sweden's most popular sport. Swedish stars play for professional teams around the world. Many people play for fun. Sweden has a good record in women's soccer, also called football. The national team won the European Championship in 1984. They have also won Olympic silver medals in 2016 and 2021. In 1988, the first professional league for women started here.

Swimmer Sarah Sjöström has won six Olympic medals, including three gold medals.

World record-holder Armand Duplantis competed for Sweden in the men's pole vault final at the 2020 Tokyo Olympics.

Ice hockey is another popular sport. Many people also play a similar sport called bandy. The rink is bigger than the one used in ice hockey. The sticks are shorter, and a ball is used instead of a puck. There are more players on a team. But many of the rules are similar.

Most Swedes love spending time outdoors. In winter, they ski and snowboard. In warmer weather, they go biking or canoeing. They also hike, fish, and swim in the lakes.

MUSIC

Sweden has a long history of music. Folk musicians play lively songs on fiddles. People perform traditional dances such as the hambo, snoa, and polska. Today, music is an important part of the school day. Sweden is famous for its pop music. The country is tied with Ireland for the most wins at the Eurovision Song Contest.

Many Swedish musicians sing in English. This helps give them a worldwide audience. ABBA, Zara Larsson, Robyn, Ace of Base, and Avicii are all from Sweden. Spotify and SoundCloud are both Swedish companies. They have changed the way we listen to music.

Swedish folk music often features a nyckelharpa. This instrument is like a large violin with keys.

BULLERIBOCK

This simple Swedish game is popular on playgrounds. You only need two people to play. And no equipment is needed!

What You Do:

1. One player turns their back to the other player. They can be standing or sitting.
2. The other player taps a rhythm on the first player's back. As they tap, they chant a rhyme in Swedish. Its words mean, "Billy goat, billy goat. How many horns stand up?"
3. At the end of the chant, they leave some of their fingertips in place.
4. The first player must guess how many fingers are on their back.

SOMETHING FOR EVERYONE

It might seem like Sweden has it all. The country is always near the top of the rankings for happiness. Swedish people value equality and balance. Their country has beautiful, wild landscapes. There are bustling cities with historic buildings. There is truly something for everyone.

GLOSSARY

alliance (uh-LY-uhnts)
an agreement between nations or groups of people to work together

Arctic Circle (ARK-tik SUR-kuhl)
an imaginary line encircling an area around the North Pole, where it is cold year-round

constitution (kahn-stuh-TOO-shuhn)
the written system of laws in a country that state the rights of people and the powers of government

economy (ee-KAH-nuh-mee)
the ways in which a country handles its money and resources

empire (EM-pire)
a group of countries ruled by a single person or government

equality (i-KWAH-luh-tee)
the same rights for everyone

glacier (GLAY-shur)
a huge moving body of ice that flows down a mountain slope or across a polar region

independent (in-di-PEN-duhnt)
free from the control of other people or things

Indigenous (in-DI-juh-nuhs)
the original inhabitants of a certain place

invade (in-VADE)
to send armed forces into another country in order to take it over

parliament (PAHR-luh-muhnt)
a group of people who make laws and run the government in some countries

procession (pruh-SESS-shuhn)
a group of people walking along in an orderly way, often for a ceremony

READ MORE

Parker, Phillip. *50 Things You Should Know About the Vikings.* Beverly, MA: Quarto Publishing, 2022.

Lombardo, Jennifer, and Joanne Mattern. *Sweden.* Buffalo, NY: Cavendish Square Publishing, 2025.

Van, R.L. *Sweden.* Minneapolis: Abdo Books, 2023.

INTERNET SITES

Britannica Kids: Sweden
kids.britannica.com/kids/article/Sweden/345794

History for Kids: The Vikings: Facts & Information for Kids
historyforkids.org/the-vikings-facts-for-kids/

National Geographic Kids: Sweden
kids.nationalgeographic.com/geography/countries/article/sweden

INDEX

ABOUT THE AUTHOR

Nancy Dickmann grew up in the United States before moving to England, where she worked as a children's book editor. She now has her dream job as a full-time author and has written more than 250 books for children, mainly on science topics. Her favorite part of the job is researching and learning new things. One highlight was getting to interview a real astronaut to find out about using the toilet in space!

SELECT BOOKS IN THIS SERIES

YOUR PASSPORT TO AUSTRALIA
YOUR PASSPORT TO BRAZIL
YOUR PASSPORT TO CUBA
YOUR PASSPORT TO EGYPT
YOUR PASSPORT TO ENGLAND
YOUR PASSPORT TO GERMANY
YOUR PASSPORT TO JAPAN
YOUR PASSPORT TO MEXICO
YOUR PASSPORT TO PORTUGAL
YOUR PASSPORT TO SAUDI ARABIA